MW00916014

100 AMAZING FACTS ABOUT MOROCCO

© 2023, Marc Dresgui

Content

"When I miss a city, I go to Marrakech"

— Yves Saint Laurent

Introduction

Welcome, dear reader, to an extraordinary journey through the mysteries, wonders and enigmas of Morocco. This country, both the cradle of ancient civilizations and a crossroads of cultures, is full of secrets and stories that have spanned the centuries. When you open this book, you are about to dive into an ocean of discoveries, where each page reveals a little-known, surprising or simply fascinating aspect of this beautiful country.

"100 Amazing Facts About Morocco" is not just a collection of anecdotes. It is an invitation to see Morocco from a different angle, to lose yourself in the maze of its medinas, to rise to the top of its majestic mountains, to let yourself be bewitched by the whispers of the Sahara. Each fact will reveal a unique facet to you, allowing you to deepen your knowledge and refine your view of this nation rich in history and culture.

So, are you ready to be surprised? With each page turned, you will be amazed, you will wonder, you will let yourself be carried away by the magic of these stories. Embark on this adventure and let yourself be guided through the 100 incredible facts that make Morocco an unforgettable country.

Marc Dresgui

Fact 1 - The Land with Two Coasts

You know, Morocco is a really special country on the world map. It is fortunate to be bordered by two large bodies of water: the Atlantic Ocean and the Mediterranean Sea. Imagine being able to swim in two different seas without having to leave the country!

To the west, the Atlantic Ocean caresses the Moroccan coast. Cities such as Agadir, Essaouira and El Jadida have long beaches where the waves crash. These beaches are popular with surfers from all over the world to face the impressive waves.

In the north, it's a completely different atmosphere. The calmer Mediterranean Sea bathes cities such as Tetouan and Al Hoceima. The waters are generally warmer, and the landscape is different with coves and cliffs in places.

So, if one day you have the opportunity to visit Morocco, don't hesitate to explore these two coasts. Each of them will reveal different treasures and experiences, like a double gift offered by nature in Morocco.

Fact 2 - The Atlas Mountains Touch the Sky

Have you ever seen a natural painting where the peaks of the mountains seem to touch the clouds? In Morocco, the Atlas mountain range gives that magical impression. It spans a large part of the country and offers breathtaking landscapes.

Mount Toubkal, for example, is the highest peak in this range and in all of North Africa. Standing at an altitude of 4,167 metres, it is like a giant watching over the country. Many adventurers come every year to try to climb it and admire the incredible view from its summit.

But the Atlas Mountains are not just a destination for mountaineers. Its green slopes, fertile valleys and traditional Berber villages offer a total change of scenery. Walking through these mountains, one can discover a multitude of cultures, traditions and landscapes.

Imagine walking along thousand-year-old paths, breathing in the pure air of the heights, while admiring panoramic views that make you feel like you're touching the sky. This is what the Moroccan Atlas has in store for you!

Fact 3 - Morocco's Mysterious Monkey

Among the fascinating creatures you can encounter in Morocco, there is a peculiar monkey called the hoard. This monkey, unlike others, does not have a tail! It is one of the only primates, along with humans, to live on the African continent without being in a jungle.

The hoard lives mainly in the Middle Atlas Mountains, and sometimes it can be seen in cedar and holm oak forests. They are very sociable and live in groups. If you have the chance to observe them, you will notice that they communicate with each other with many sounds and gestures.

But what's even more astonishing is that the hoard is one of the few monkeys to live so far north on the African continent. Despite climate change and threats from humans, this monkey has managed to survive in these areas for thousands of years.

If one day you go for a walk in the Moroccan mountains, keep your eyes peeled! Maybe you'll be lucky enough to come across this mysterious monkey and admire its acrobatics between the branches.

Fact 4 - The Tree That Yields Precious Oil

In Morocco, there is a truly special tree that holds a treasure: the argan tree. Its fruits contain nuts, and inside these nuts, there is an oil of great value, argan oil. Maybe you've heard of it before?

This oil is appreciated all over the world for its benefits. In cooking, it adds a unique flavor to dishes and is rich in vitamins. But that's not all. It is also very popular for skin and hair care, thanks to its moisturizing and nourishing properties.

What makes argan oil even more special is its rarity. The argan tree grows only in certain regions of Morocco, mainly between Agadir, Essaouira and Taroudant. For generations, Berber women have developed a unique know-how to extract this oil by hand, a delicate work that requires patience and precision.

So, the next time you use or hear about argan oil, remember this amazing tree and the expert hands that helped create this Moroccan wonder.

Fact 5 - The Berbers, the first Moroccans

Long before Morocco was called "Morocco", it was inhabited by a proud and ancient people: the Berbers. You know, they're the true natives of this land and have a history that goes back thousands of years.

The Berbers have left fascinating traces of their passage. Have you ever seen those ancient rock carvings depicting animals and scenes of life? They are the work of the Berbers, and can be found in the Sahara and the Atlas Mountains. It's like a photo album carved in stone that tells us their story.

Over time, the Berbers created powerful kingdoms, built impressive citadels, and developed a unique language and culture. This language, Tamazight, is still spoken today by many Moroccans, and it even has its own alphabet, called Tifinagh.

When you hear about Morocco, remember that its soul is Berber. These early Moroccans shaped the country and continue to do so with their traditions, language, and incredible heritage.

Fact 6 - The university is older than the Sorbonne

Have you ever heard of the Sorbonne in Paris, one of the most famous universities in the world? Well, did you know that Morocco is home to an even older university? Its name is Al-Qarawiyyin, located in Fez, and it is a real treasure of history.

Founded in 859 by Fatima al-Fihri, an educated Berber woman, Al-Qarawiyyin is recognized by UNESCO and the Guinness Book of World Records as the oldest continuously operating university in the world. Impressive, isn't it?

Since its inception, the university has attracted students and scholars from all over the world. They came to learn and debate on various subjects such as theology, astronomy, music and medicine. Some of the greatest Muslim thinkers, such as Ibn Khaldun, studied or taught there.

So, the next time you think of great universities, don't forget about Al-Qarawiyyin in Fez. It is a place of knowledge that has shone for more than a millennium and shows how Morocco has always been at the crossroads of civilizations and cultures.

Fact 7 - Mohammed VI, the 23rd Alawite King

Have you ever heard of the kings who have marked the history of a country? In Morocco, the Alaouite dynasty has ruled for centuries. And do you know who the 23rd king of this line is? It's Mohammed VI. A modern king, with a vision for the future.

Born in 1963, Mohammed VI ascended the throne in 1999, succeeding his father Hassan II. Since his accession, he has introduced several important reforms, with the ambition of modernising the country while respecting its traditions. For example, he worked for women's rights and the modernization of the economy.

One of the great achievements of his reign is the new Constitution adopted in 2011. This constitution strengthened democracy, gave more powers to the parliament and guaranteed more rights to Moroccan citizens.

So, when we talk about modern Morocco, we can't ignore the role of Mohammed VI. As the 23rd Alawite king, he continues the legacy of his dynasty while paving the way for a progressive and forward-looking Morocco.

Fact 8 - One Battle, Three Kings

Imagine a gigantic battle where not one, not two, but three kings are present on the battlefield. Sounds amazing, doesn't it? And yet, it happened in Morocco during the famous Battle of the Three Kings in 1578.

This battle, also known as the Battle of Ksar El Kebir, saw three armies led by three monarchs face each other. On the one hand, there was the young king of Portugal, Sebastian I, who dreamed of military glory. On the other, two pretenders to the Moroccan throne: Sultan Abd al-Malik and his nephew, Moulay Ahmed.

The battle was fierce, but at the end of the day, the result was shocking. All three kings died in this confrontation, making this clash a unique event in world history. Morocco emerged victorious, consolidating its sovereignty and pushing back against European influence.

Whenever you hear about great historical battles, remember Ksar El Kebir. A place where three kings clashed, forever changing the course of the history of Morocco and Europe.

Fact 9 - Colorful markets called "souks"

Have you ever dreamed of walking through a place where every nook and cranny is filled with mesmerizing colors, smells and sounds? Welcome to the souks of Morocco! These traditional markets are at the heart of city life and immerse you in a fascinating world.

As soon as you enter a souk, your senses are engaged. The scents of spices waft through the air, taking you on a journey through exotic flavors like saffron, cumin or cinnamon. Around you, you can see stalls overflowing with handicrafts: hand-woven rugs, chiseled copper lamps, sparkling jewelry.

But a souk is not just a place to buy. It is also a social space where people meet, discuss and negotiate. If you look closely, you'll see craftsmen at work, creating beautiful objects before your eyes, or musicians playing catchy melodies.

So, the next time you hear about markets, think about the Moroccan souks. Magical places that let you experience the authenticity and cultural richness of a country with every step you take.

Fact 10 - Gnaoua music with haunting rhythms

Close your eyes and imagine yourself being lulled by deep rhythms, powerful chants and hypnotic dances. This is what it is like to experience Gnaoua music, a unique musical tradition of Morocco.

This music has its roots in sub-Saharan Africa, but it has taken a special form in Morocco, where it has been influenced by Berber, Arab and Andalusian cultures. The key instruments are the guembri, a kind of lute, and the krakebs, metal castanets. These instruments give Gnaoua music its distinct sound.

But Gnaoua music is not just a melody for the ears. It is also spiritual, often used in healing ceremonies. The musicians, called "Maâlems", and dancers often go into a trance, connecting to a spiritual world.

Next time you're looking for music that transports you, think of the Gnaoua music of Morocco. It is the expression of a rich history, a fusion of cultures and a deep spirituality, all wrapped in rhythms that captivate the soul.

Fact 11 - Friday Couscous

Did you know that couscous, a delicious semolina dish with vegetables, meat or fish, has a special meaning in Morocco? Indeed, in this country, Friday couscous is a tradition that many cherish.

In Morocco, Friday is considered a holy day, similar to what Sunday represents in many Christian countries. After the big Friday prayer, families gather to share a communal meal, and the star dish is often couscous. It is a time of communion, sharing and gratitude.

Preparing couscous is an art in itself. The semolina is carefully steamed, the vegetables and meat are slowly simmered to release all their flavors. And each family has its own secret recipe, passed down from generation to generation.

So, the next time you're enjoying couscous, think of those Moroccan families who get together every Friday. For them, it's not just a dish, but a celebration of family, faith and tradition.

Fact 12 - Tagine, a stew like no other

Imagine a special terracotta pot with a conical lid that contains exceptional flavours. This pot is called tagine, and the dish it prepares has the same name. Unique to Morocco, tagine is a tasty stew that makes foodies from all over the world salivate.

Inside this pot, simple ingredients turn into a delicious dish. Meats, vegetables, spices, and sometimes dried fruits or olives, simmer gently, letting each component infuse the other. The secret? The shape of the tagine's lid allows the steam to circulate and fall, keeping the dish juicy and rich in flavor.

There are countless variations of tagine, from mild to spicy, sweet to savory. Some contain chicken with candied lemon and olives, others mutton with plums and almonds. Every region, every family has its own favorite version.

The next time you have the opportunity to taste a tagine, remember its long history and the richness of Moroccan cuisine. A taste journey awaits you with every bite!

Fact 13 - Imilchil Moussem, Wedding Festival

Have you ever heard of a place where dozens of couples get married at the same time, in the middle of a big festival? This is what happens in Imilchil, a village located in the Atlas Mountains in Morocco, during the Moussem d'Imilchil.

This is no ordinary wedding, it is a celebration that lasts three days and attracts thousands of people! In the past, it was an opportunity for young Berbers from different tribes to meet and choose a partner for life. Today, although many couples are already engaged before the Moussem, the festival continues to celebrate love and union.

But Imilchil's Moussem isn't just about weddings. It is also a large fair where people exchange goods, chat, play music and dance. Berber traditions are proudly represented through songs, dances and colorful costumes.

If one day you have the chance to visit Morocco during the Moussem of Imilchil, you will discover a fascinating tradition that mixes love, culture and festivities, in the heart of the majestic Atlas Mountains.

Fact 14 - Two Eid for a great country

In Morocco, as in many Muslim countries, there are two major holidays that everyone looks forward to: Eid al-Fitr and Eid al-Adha. These holidays are called "Eid," which means "feast" or "celebration" in Arabic.

Eid al-Fitr, often referred to as "Little Eid," takes place at the end of the holy month of Ramadan. After a month of fasting, from sunrise to sunset, it's a time to rejoice, share delicious meals, and give each other gifts. The streets come alive, families come together and children put on their best clothes.

Eid al-Adha, also known as the "Great Eid," commemorates Abraham's sacrifice. It is a festival of sharing where a sheep is traditionally sacrificed. The meat is then distributed among family, neighbors, and those in need.

In Morocco, these two Eids are highlights of the year. They remind us of the importance of family, sharing and generosity. If you visit Morocco during one of these Eids, you will feel the effervescence and joy that animates the country during these celebrations.

Fact 15 - Berber Desert Fridges

Imagine a place where the scorching sun is omnipresent and the heat can be oppressive. This is the case in many parts of Morocco, especially in the desert. But did you know that even under these conditions, the Berbers found an ingenious way to keep their food cool?

The Berbers, the indigenous inhabitants of Morocco, invented natural "fridges", called "zeers". These clay pots, made up of two different sized pots, one inside the other, use evaporation to cool their contents. The space between the two pots is filled with wet sand, which evaporates and cools the inside of the inner pot.

These zeers do not require electricity or mechanical parts. It is an eco-friendly and sustainable solution for keeping food, such as fruits and vegetables, away from the heat of the desert. Thanks to these jars, food can stay fresh for several days!

So, the next time you're complaining about the heat, think about the ingenuity of the Berbers and their natural fridges that help them survive in one of the hottest environments on the planet.

Fact 16 - Chefchaouen, the blue city

Have you ever dreamed of a city where almost everything is painted blue? Chefchaouen, nestled in the Rif Mountains in Morocco, is exactly that magical place. Every street corner, staircase and building is tinted with different shades of blue, from pastel skies to deep blues.

But why this color? There are several stories circulating. Some say blue repels mosquitoes. Others believe it is reminiscent of heaven and paradise, creating a spiritual atmosphere. And there are also those who believe that blue, by reflecting the sun, keeps homes cooler during the warm months.

As you walk through its narrow alleys, you will feel a sense of calm and serenity. The blue shadows play on the cobblestones, creating an almost unreal atmosphere. And when you look up, you'll often see majestic mountains framing this picturesque picture.

So, if you are looking for a unique place in the world, where time seems to have stopped and where everything is imbued with poetry, think of Chefchaouen, the blue pearl of Morocco.

Fact 17 - Ibn Battuta, the Traveler from Tangier

Imagine a traveler, starting from his hometown, traveling the world for almost 30 years! This incredible man was Ibn Battuta. Born in Tangier, Morocco, in 1304, he became one of the greatest explorers in history, long before Christopher Columbus or Marco Polo.

His insatiable curiosity has driven him to travel throughout Africa, Asia and even Europe. During his adventures, he visited places such as Mecca, India, China, and many more. Wherever he went, he took the time to jot down his observations, describing the cultures, people, and wonders he encountered.

His writings, collected in a book called "Rihla" (which means "Journey"), are a valuable source for historians. They offer a unique insight into the societies and civilizations of his time. Thanks to him, we know much more about the medieval world.

So, if you love adventure and discovery, let yourself be inspired by Ibn Battuta. His courage and thirst for knowledge have made him a true legend in Morocco and around the world.

Fact 18 - Stars and constellations in Marrakech

Have you ever rolled your eyes on a clear night in Marrakech? This city, with its starry nights, is a real treasure trove for astronomy enthusiasts. For centuries, the Moroccan sky has fascinated not only poets and dreamers, but also scientists.

The ancient inhabitants of Marrakech used the stars to guide themselves on their journeys through the desert. The constellations were like celestial maps, helping caravans find their way through the vastness of the dunes. But that wasn't all. The stars also had spiritual significance, connecting humans to the universe.

Today, modern observatories are set up in Marrakech to study the sky. Thanks to them, we learn more about the mysteries of the universe, from black holes to distant galaxies. These observatories attract astronomers from all over the world, who come to study the sky without light pollution.

So, next time you're in Marrakech, don't forget to look up. Who knows, maybe you'll discover a new star or constellation you've never seen before!

Fact 19 - Aït-Benhaddou, a village from another time

Have you ever dreamed of traveling back in time? Aït-Benhaddou, a village located in Morocco, gives you the unique feeling of being in a world of yesteryear. The ochre earthen buildings, clinging to a hill, seem to have remained unchanged for centuries.

This fortified village, or ksar, is made up of traditional houses built of adobe, a technique that uses clay mixed with water and straw. These houses, with their decorative towers, are connected by narrow streets that wind along the hill. You can almost hear the echoes of the merchants and craftsmen of yesteryear!

Aït-Benhaddou is not only a jewel of Moroccan heritage. It has also been the setting for many films and TV series, seduced by its ancient charm. It's as if this village is an open door to history.

When you visit Aït-Benhaddou, you understand why it is a UNESCO World Heritage Site. It's a magical place where time seems to stand still, allowing you to connect with Moroccan history and culture.

Fact 20 - Hercules, the hero at the Moroccan cave

Have you ever heard of the legends related to Hercules, the hero of Greek mythology known for his extraordinary strength and twelve labors? But did you know that his name is also linked to a mystical cave in Morocco?

This cave, located near Tangier, is called "The Caves of Hercules". According to legend, after completing his twelve labors, Hercules came to rest in this cave, hiding from the outside world. If you look closely at the entrance to the cave, it looks like an inverted silhouette of Africa, fueling the imagination of locals and visitors alike.

But that's not all. Some local legends say that it was in these caves that Hercules separated Africa from Europe by digging the Strait of Gibraltar. Standing there, you can almost feel the power of myth, history mixed with reality.

During your visit, let yourself be carried away by the magic of the place, the tales of the past and the roar of the waves. The Cave of Hercules is more than just a cavity in the rock: it's a journey through time and mythology.

Fact 21 - The saffron fields of Taliouine

Have you ever tasted a dish or drink flavored with saffron? This reddish spice is as precious as gold, and it has its origins in a special place in Morocco: Taliouine.

Lost in the heart of the Atlas Mountains, the Taliouine plateau is the Moroccan epicentre of saffron cultivation. It is in this little corner of paradise that the flowers of Crocus sativus grow, giving rise to these precious red filaments. If you had the opportunity to go in autumn, you would witness the saffron picking, a delicate ritual carried out by hand, early in the morning to preserve the freshness of the flower.

But why Taliouine? Thanks to its unique climate and fertile soil, this region offers the ideal conditions to produce saffron of exceptional quality. You can even take part in workshops to discover the process of transforming this spice, from the field to your plate.

The next time you enjoy a saffron dish, think of Taliouine, its purple fields and the delicacy of the hands that made this experience possible.

Fact 22 - The Desert Caravans of Olden

Have you ever dreamed of vast expanses of sand, dunes undulating in the scorching sun and majestic camels marching in single file? If so, you visualize the fascinating picture of the desert caravans that once crisscrossed the Sahara.

Caravans were much more than just convoys of goods. They embodied the vital network of trade and communication between North Africa and sub-Saharan Africa. As you delve into the story, you'll discover that these trips were no small feat. Facing sandstorms, thirst, and the vastness of the desert, merchants transported salt, gold, ivory, and slaves over long distances.

The oases dotted in the desert were life-saving stopovers for these caravans. These watering holes and greenery allowed travellers and their animals to rest and refuel before continuing their journey. Cities like Timbuktu in Mali have become prosperous thanks to their strategic position on these trade routes.

Imagine the twilight over the desert, the sound of camels, the songs of merchants by the fireside. These caravans embody a bygone but fascinating era in the history of the Maghreb.

Fact 23 - The Dromedary, King of the Sands

When you think of the desert, what is the first image that comes to mind? For many, it is that of the dromedary, that majestic one-humped animal, perfectly adapted to the arid life of the desert.

The dromedary has a series of fascinating adaptations that allow it to survive in extreme conditions. For example, you'd be surprised to learn that its hump doesn't contain water, contrary to popular belief, but is actually a fat reserve. This fat can be converted into water and energy when resources are scarce.

These creatures are also incredible heat resistant. Their body temperature can fluctuate in order to avoid sweating during the day. And when you see a camel drinking, know that it can swallow up to 40 liters of water in a few minutes!

Throughout the ages, the dromedary has been an essential companion for the people of the desert. Not only as a means of transportation, but also as a source of food, milk and wool. So it's no wonder he's nicknamed the "King of the Sands."

Fact 24 - The ancient art of Berber weaving

Maybe you've already admired these rugs with geometric patterns and bright colors in a home or museum. These works, witnesses of ancestral know-how, are the expression of the art of Berber weaving.

The Berbers, an indigenous people of North Africa, have passed on this art from generation to generation, making weaving much more than just a craft: a tradition, a language. Each pattern, each color tells a story, a rite or a belief. For example, the diamond symbol is often associated with the protective eye, offering security and benevolence.

Weaving techniques vary, but most rugs are made from sheep's wool. Berber women, the main artisans of this art, use natural dyes to bring their creations to life. Their craftsmanship is such that a single rug can require several months of hard work.

So, the next time you come across one of these Berber rugs, remember that it is not just a decorative object, but a page of history, woven with passion and dedication.

Fact 25 - A mosque whose minaret touches the sky

If you look up at the sky in Casablanca, you can't miss this architectural marvel that seems to touch the clouds: the Hassan II Mosque. With its minaret rising to 210 meters, it is the tallest in Africa, and it stands proudly, testifying to human ingenuity and spiritual greatness.

Inaugurated in 1993, this mosque is one of the few in Morocco open to non-Muslims. It can accommodate more than 105,000 worshippers, making it one of the largest mosques in the world. Its intricately crafted doors, carved ceilings, and detailed mosaics reflect Moroccan craftsmanship.

What is even more impressive is the part of the mosque built on the water. It has a sunroof and offers stunning views of the Atlantic. Legend has it that the mosque fulfilled King Hassan II's wish to "build a mosque on water, for the throne of God is on water".

On your next visit to Casablanca, take a moment to admire this wonder. It is the symbol of the successful marriage between tradition and modernity.

Fact 26 - The Magic of Henna

Henna, that greenish powder that turns into a reddish or brownish hue when applied to the skin, is much more than just a dye. In Morocco, as in many cultures, henna is shrouded in traditions, symbols, and stories.

For centuries, Moroccan women have used henna to adorn their hands and feet with intricate designs during ceremonies or special moments. A wedding, for example, wouldn't be complete without the bride showing off an elaborately crafted henna design, which is supposed to bring her luck and happiness.

But henna isn't just for joyful occasions. It is also used for its healing properties. You may not have known that Berbers apply it to relieve headaches or joint pain. Henna naturally cools the body, making it a valuable remedy in hot regions.

The next time you see these beautiful henna designs, remember that they're not just aesthetically pleasing. They reflect a rich culture, deep history and ancestral traditions.

Fact 27 - The sea of sand in Merzouga

When you think of Morocco, you may picture bustling markets and ancient cities. However, in Merzouga, a completely different picture emerges: an endless sea of golden dunes stretching as far as the eye can see. Located at the gateway to the Sahara, Merzouga is famous for its majestic dunes, among the highest in Morocco.

Erg Chebbi, as it is called, offers a unique sensory experience. The silence is almost palpable, broken only by the breath of the wind or the slow step of a dromedary. If you have the opportunity to spend the night there, you will discover a starry sky of unimaginable clarity, far from any light pollution.

It's not just a place of wonder for tourists. For the locals, the desert is both a source of life and a challenge. They have adapted their way of life to this extreme environment, taking advantage of limited resources while respecting the fragility of the ecosystem.

So, if one day you stand on top of a dune in Merzouga, take a moment to breathe deeply and feel the magic of the desert. You will be in the heart of a sea of sand, silent witness to a thousand and one stories.

Fact 28 - The Secret Gardens of Marrakech

In the heart of Marrakech's noisy and bustling medina, you might be surprised to discover true oases of tranquility: the hidden gardens. These havens of peace, often nestled behind high terracotta walls, are architectural and horticultural treasures, witnesses to the city's rich past.

One of the most emblematic is the Jardin Majorelle. Created by French artist Jacques Majorelle and later owned by renowned designer Yves Saint Laurent, this garden is a magical fusion of exotic plants, ponds and buildings painted in an intense blue. Its beauty is sure to captivate you.

But it's not just the Jardin Majorelle. Other green spaces, such as the Badii Garden or the Agdal Garden, tell you stories of royal love, lavish parties and spiritual connections. Their design reflects the ancient Moroccan gardeners' mastery of water management, a valuable element in this region.

If you get lost in the alleys of Marrakech, don't hesitate to push open the door of a garden. You may find the secret soul of this enchanting city.

Fact 29 - The secrets of the hammam

Have you ever wondered what makes the hammam so special and popular? This ancient bathing ritual, steeped in Middle Eastern and North African culture, is much more than just a spa experience. It is a journey for the senses, combining tradition, relaxation and purification.

At the heart of the hammam is the steam room. The enveloping moisture opens the pores and prepares the skin for the traditional scrub. This is where the "kessa", a rough glove, comes into play. By using it, you'll get rid of dead skin cells, revealing soft, renewed skin underneath. You may have heard of black soap, a paste made from crushed black olives and oil, which is essential in this process.

But the hammam is more than just body purification. It is also a place for socializing, where people gather to chat, laugh and share precious moments. In the past, it was a key place for communities, a place for exchange and news.

If the opportunity arises, don't hesitate to dive into this thousand-year-old tradition. You will not only come out refreshed, but also imbued with the essence of an ancestral practice.

Fact 30 - Arabic calligraphy, a Moroccan art

Have you ever taken the time to admire the beauty of the curves and patterns of Arabic calligraphy? This refined art, deeply rooted in Moroccan culture, is much more than just writing. It is an artistic expression, a dance of letters that tells stories and conveys emotions.

Arabic calligraphy developed from the writing of the Qur'an, the holy book of Islam. Over time, it has become an art form in its own right. In Moroccan palaces and mosques, you can often observe verses from the Quran delicately inscribed on the walls, testifying to the marriage of spirituality and art.

But this practice is not limited to places of worship. It extends to other fields, such as interior design, henna tattoos, and even contemporary art. Modern Moroccan artists often incorporate calligraphy into their works, merging tradition and modernity.

The next time you visit Morocco or see a piece of calligraphy, take a moment to appreciate it. It's an opportunity to connect with an ancient tradition that continues to live and flourish.

Fact 31 - The Festival of Roses in Kelâat M'Gouna

Can you imagine a sea of roses stretching as far as the eye can see? Every year in May, the valley of Kelâat M'Gouna, in Morocco, is transformed into an ocean fragrant with pink petals. This is the time of year when the famous Rose Festival takes place, an event that celebrates the blooming of Damascena roses.

The festival lasts three days and is an explosion of color, scents, and joy. The streets come alive with parades, songs and dances, and the locals dress up in their best traditional clothes. The roses, of course, are the real stars. They adorn every nook and cranny of the city, in the form of garlands, bouquets or even wreaths.

These roses are not only beautiful, they are also very useful. Kelâat M'Gouna is renowned for its production of rose water, which is used in cosmetics and gastronomy. During the festival, you can visit local distilleries and learn about the process of making this fragrant elixir.

So, if you have the opportunity to visit Morocco in the spring, don't miss this unique celebration. The Rose Festival is an incomparable sensory experience that will immerse you in the heart of Berber culture.

Fact 32 - Tales of the Medina

Have you ever wandered through the winding alleys of a Moroccan medina? If so, you've surely felt the mystical atmosphere here, where every street corner seems to tell an ancient story. For centuries, the medinas have been the cradles of Moroccan tales and legends.

These tales, passed down from generation to generation, come to life at night, when storytellers gather in public squares. With captivating voices and theatrical gestures, they tell stories of heroes, jinns, love and betrayal, captivating the audience until the last word.

In addition to their entertaining value, these tales have a social function. They convey life lessons, moral values and strengthen community bonds. For example, the story of "Aisha Kandicha", a seductive but evil female spirit, teaches caution and respect for traditions.

So, the next time you visit a medina, keep your ears open as night falls. Let yourself be carried away by these immemorial tales that will immerse you in the deep soul of Morocco and remind you of the timeless magic of storytelling.

Fact 33 - The fishermen of Essaouira

Essaouira, with its mesmerizing charm, is much more than just a tourist destination on the Moroccan coast. As you walk along its ramparts, you will quickly see the fishermen, the true souls of this port city, busy with their daily tasks.

Every morning, when the sun is just beginning to emerge, these brave men set sail in their blue boats, defying the waves in search of the day's fish. They carry within them an ancestral knowledge, inherited from their ancestors, which guides them in this daily dance with the ocean.

When they return, the port comes alive with incredible energy. The merchants, the shouts of the auctions, the smell of fresh fish; Everything blends together in a mosaic of sounds and smells. If you dare to try their catch, you will discover an unparalleled freshness, whether it is grilled sardines or squid in sauce.

Behind every fish sold is a story, a work, a passion. By soaking up this atmosphere, you pay tribute to these fishermen of Essaouira, guardians of traditions and pillars of their community.

Fact 34 - Fossils of the Sahara

Did you know that the vast Sahara Desert wasn't always the arid landscape you see today? Indeed, there was a time when this desert was submerged under water, providing a rich and varied habitat for many marine organisms.

During your travels in Morocco, you might be surprised to come across fossils in the middle of the desert. These prehistoric remains are silent witnesses of a bygone era, when the Sahara was a seabed teeming with life. From trilobites to ammonites, the diversity of fossils discovered is impressive.

From markets to dedicated workshops, Morocco has been able to make the most of this unique paleontological richness. In Erfoud, for example, you can discover specialized workshops where craftsmen work these fossilized stones to create beautiful art and decorative objects.

When you look at these fossils, you get to know the history of our planet, a history that goes back millions of years. These treasures of the past, buried under the Saharan sands, remind us of the constant evolution of the Earth and the magic of nature.

Fact 35 - Imider's Silver Treasure

Have you ever heard of the small village of Imider, nestled in the Atlas Mountains in Morocco? This village, at first glance ordinary, holds a precious secret: it is located close to one of the largest silver mines in the world.

For decades, Imider's mines have been producing an impressive amount of silver, making Morocco one of the world's leading producers of this precious metal. This subterranean treasure has, over time, shaped the lives of the inhabitants, linking them unbreakably to the land that offers them so much.

However, this wealth is not without consequences. The mine, while providing economic opportunities, has also posed environmental and social challenges. Residents of Imider have sometimes protested, voicing concerns about water use and the ecological impact of mining.

When you visit Imider, you witness the duality of human nature in the face of wealth. On the one hand, the shiny brilliance of silver and, on the other, the challenges of its quest. A story of hidden treasures and complex realities.

Fact 36 - The natural bridge of Imi n'Ifri

Have you ever dreamed of seeing a natural bridge sculpted by time itself? Let me introduce you to Imi n'Ifri, a stunning natural phenomenon located not far from Demnate, Morocco. This bridge, the result of millennia of erosion, seems to have been designed by an artist's hand rather than by nature.

As you get closer, you notice that the bridge connects two mountains, forming a majestic arch over a river. The play of light and shadow, combined with the soothing sounds of flowing water, creates a living tableau, harmoniously blending the elements of earth and water.

But that's not all. The walls of this rock formation are adorned with cave paintings, silent testimonies of the peoples who inhabited the area thousands of years ago. These drawings add a historical dimension to the natural beauty of the place.

If you ever go to Morocco, don't miss out on this natural wonder. Imi n'Ifri is a true ode to the eternal beauty of nature and the deep history of the country.

Fact 37 - The Mysterious Library of Fez

Have you ever heard of the Al-Qarawiyyin Library in Fez? It is not only the oldest working library, but also one of Morocco's most precious cultural treasures. Founded in the 9th century, this library is as old as the city itself.

As you walk through its doors, you are immediately enveloped by a solemn atmosphere, where the weight of the centuries is felt. The shelves are full of rare manuscripts, some of which are unique in the world, dealing with theology, medicine and astronomy. Among them is an original version by the famous historian Ibn Khaldun.

It is not only a place of learning, but also an architectural masterpiece. The delicate motifs, carved columns, and intricately crafted wooden ceilings reflect the refinement of Islamic art of the time. Every nook and cranny tells a story, every wall whispers secrets of the past.

So, if you're looking to delve into the depths of Moroccan history and get a feel for the greatness of Islamic civilization, the Al-Qarawiyyin Library is a must-stop during your visit to Fez.

Fact 38 - The camel, cousin of the dromedary

Did you know that the camel and the dromedary are often confused, even though they are two distinct species? While the dromedary, typical of the North African regions, has only one hump, its cousin the camel, native to Central Asia, proudly sports two on its back.

These bumps are not filled with water as some believe. Instead, they store fat, allowing these animals to survive for days or even weeks without food. This energy reserve is particularly useful when they travel long distances in arid and hostile environments.

Although their habitats are far apart, these two animals share common characteristics that make them adapted to life in the desert. Thick eyelids protect them from sandstorms, and their wide feet prevent them from sinking into the hot sand.

So, the next time you come across one of these majestic animals in the desert or in a documentary, you'll be able to tell the camel from the camel and admire the wonderful adaptations that allow them to master the challenges of the desert.

Fact 39 - Fint's Oasis, Jewel of the Desert

In the heart of the Moroccan desert, you will find a real natural treasure: the oasis of Fint. Nestled between high mountains and surrounded by rock formations, this oasis is a haven of greenery that contrasts with the surrounding aridity. The water meanders smoothly, nourishing the vegetation and bringing life to this remote region.

For centuries, local people have made Fint a place to live, exploiting its resources to grow date palms, almond trees, and other fruit trees. These plantations not only provide a source of food, but also shade and refuge from the relentless desert heat.

If you venture to Fint, you'll be amazed by the contrast between the green of the palm trees and the brown of the mountains. The locals, welcoming and warm, will gladly tell you the stories and legends that surround this magical place.

All in all, Fint's Oasis is a vivid reminder that, even in the most arid and desolate places, nature always finds a way to flourish. If you're looking for a moment of peace away from the hustle and bustle, this is the place to be.

Fact 40 - Morocco's Round Bread

If you visit Morocco, you will quickly notice a constant in the meals: round bread, or "khobz" in Arabic. This thick and fluffy patty is much more than just a food, it is a symbol of Moroccan culture and tradition.

Produced from wheat flour, water, yeast and salt, khobz is distinguished by its golden rind and tender interior. Each household has its own version, with variations depending on the region. But the ritual remains the same: knead, let it rest, then bake. It's not just its flavor that makes it special, but also its role. In Morocco, bread is often used as a utensil for searing food, especially in tagines or salads.

Sharing bread is an act of hospitality and communion. When you are invited to someone's home, you will often be presented with a whole loaf of bread, a sign of generosity and respect. It's a gesture that strengthens the bonds between the guests.

Thus, khobz is not just a simple accompaniment. It is the reflection of a history, an identity and a know-how that endures through the generations.

Fact 41 - The Magic Potion in the Teapot

As soon as you set foot in Morocco, you are immediately greeted by the warmth of its people and the bewitching aroma of its emblematic drink: mint tea. Often referred to as the "green gold" of the country, this drink is much more than just a refreshment, it is the heart of Moroccan traditions.

Concocted from green tea, sugar and fresh mint, this decoction is carefully prepared in a metal teapot. Each step of its preparation is a ritual, from the infusion to the way the tea is poured high to aerate the drink and form a fine foam on the surface. It is not uncommon to see this gesture repeated several times to get the perfect mixture.

But beyond its preparation, mint tea is also a symbol of conviviality and hospitality. Whether it is shared with friends, family or strangers, it is always a moment of exchange and communion.

So, the next time you find yourself in front of a steaming pot of tea in Morocco, know that you're enjoying much more than just a drink. You share a magic potion, woven with stories and traditions.

Fact 42 - Warriors of the Desert

As you explore the vast expanses of the Moroccan desert, you might hear echoes of legendary warriors who once roamed these arid lands: the Desert Warriors. These men, mostly belonging to nomadic Berber tribes, were adapted to a life of resilience and bravery under extreme conditions.

Armed with sharp swords and mounted on sturdy camels, they mastered the art of war in the desert. The strategic use of the dunes as shelters, as well as their knowledge of oases and waterholes, allowed them to have an advantage over their opponents. Their fame was such that they were said to be as elusive as the wind of the desert.

But these warriors weren't just fighters. They were also the guardians of the trans-Saharan trade routes, ensuring the safety of the cargo caravans that crossed the desert.

So, as you gaze out over the golden dunes of the Sahara, imagine the shadows of these desert warriors, riding proudly and watching over the secrets and treasures of these mysterious lands.

Fact 43 - The Silver Jewels of the Amazigh

While walking around Morocco, you may have noticed these shiny silver jewels proudly worn by Amazigh women. These ornaments are not only aesthetically pleasing, they tell a rich and complex history of Berber culture.

Each piece is unique and handcrafted by local artisans, and serves to express the wearer's identity, social status, and region of origin. For example, a bracelet adorned with geometric symbols may evoke mountains or valleys, reflecting the natural environment in which it was designed.

The materials, mainly silver, are carefully chosen, as they possess spiritual significance. Money, in particular, is believed to offer protection from the evil eye and ward off evil spirits.

So, the next time you admire an Amazigh silver necklace or ring, remember that you are holding in your hands much more than just a piece of jewelry: it is a fragment of the soul and history of a thousand-year-old people.

Fact 44 - The Enigma of the Kasbah

Have you ever heard of the kasbahs, these majestic terracotta fortresses that stand out in the landscapes of Morocco? These structures, often perched on hills or in the heart of oases, hold secrets that are lost in the twists and turns of time.

Initially, kasbahs were built by local tribes to defend themselves against invasions. These fortresses also served as residences for local lords. Inside, you'd find expansive courtyards, cool rooms, and mazes of passageways, designed to disorient potential intruders.

But what is most astonishing is the ability of these buildings to stand the test of time. Despite the elements, many of them remain intact, testifying to the architectural mastery of the Berber builders. Their thick walls provide insulation against the summer heat and winter cold.

The next time you stand in front of a kasbah, think of all the tales it has seen, the generations it has sheltered, and the riddles it still holds within its walls.

Fact 45 - The Hidden Valleys of Morocco

Do you know the hidden treasures of Morocco? Beyond its bustling cities and arid deserts, the country is home to secret valleys of breathtaking beauty. These places, imbued with tranquility, offer a natural spectacle worthy of the most beautiful postcards.

Among them, the Valley of Roses, near Kelaat M'Gouna, would invite you to a fragrant walk, especially in spring, when the roses are in full bloom. There, the locals carry on the tradition of distilling these flowers to produce essences and fragrant waters.

Another gem, the Draa Valley, winds along the Draa River, between the High Atlas and the Anti-Atlas. As you walk through it, you will discover green palm groves juxtaposed with arid terrains, and ancient kasbahs dominating the landscape.

Finally, for mountain lovers, the Aït Bouguemez Valley, nicknamed "the Happy Valley", offers spectacular mountain panoramas. So, are you ready to explore these hidden wonders? Morocco awaits you, with its valleys full of mysteries and stories to tell.

Fact 46 - The Dance of the Horses in Fez

Have you ever heard of the majestic dance of the horses in Fez? In this thousand-year-old city, a unique equestrian tradition has been perpetuated for centuries, mixing art, history and culture.

In Fez, during some ceremonies, you might witness the "Tbourida" or "Fantasia", an equestrian demonstration where riders, dressed in traditional costumes, perform both coordinated and spectacular charges. These synchronized movements of horses and riders resemble an elegant and powerful dance, to the sound of gunpowder guns resounding in the air.

But there's more to this dance than just equestrian prowess. It also symbolizes the courage, honor and know-how of Moroccan riders. This tradition, passed down from generation to generation, is a testament to the deep connection between the Moroccan people and their horses.

If you ever visit Fez for one of these celebrations, take a moment to admire this mesmerizing dance. You will surely let yourself be carried away by the magic and heritage of this ancestral tradition.

Fact 47 - The Rite of Mint Tea

Have you ever tasted Moroccan mint tea? More than just a drink, it is a real social rite, a symbol of hospitality and conviviality in Morocco.

The preparation of this tea is an art in itself. First, green tea, usually of the Gunpowder type, is poured into it. Then, fresh mint leaves and large amounts of sugar are added. The mixture is then brought to a boil. What really sets this preparation apart is the act of pouring the tea from a height, creating a foam on the surface of each glass.

But that's not all. Serving tea is also a ritual. The master of the house usually pours it three times for each guest, each glass having its own meaning: the first is bitter as life, the second is strong as love, and the third is sweet as death.

The next time you're treated to a glass of mint tea on your trip to Morocco, remember everything behind this tradition. It is an invitation to share a moment, a history and a culture.

Fact 48 - The Monumental Gates of Meknes

Have you ever heard of the majestic gates of Meknes? This Moroccan imperial city, often less mentioned than its sisters Marrakech and Fez, contains incomparable architectural treasures, and its gates are a striking example of this.

One of the most famous is Bab Mansour, considered one of the largest and most beautiful gates in all of Morocco. Adorned with green zelliges and massive columns, it is a testament to the architectural genius of Sultan Moulay Ismail. As you walk through this door, you are transported directly into the history and refinement of the time.

But Bab Mansour is not alone. Meknes has several other equally impressive gates, each with its own history and significance. They were both strategic access points to the city and symbols of power and protection.

On your next visit to Meknes, take the time to admire these monumental gates. Each stone, each mosaic, tells a part of the rich and complex history of this imperial city.

Fact 49 - Quranic Schools of the Past

Do you know the importance of Koranic schools in the history of the Maghreb? In the past, these institutions, called "madrasas", were at the heart of the transmission of knowledge and education in the Muslim world.

These madrassas were much more than just schools. They were centers of learning where students came to memorize the Qur'an, but also to study Islamic jurisprudence, grammar, rhetoric, and other scientific and literary disciplines. For example, the Bou Inania Madrasa in Fez is a 14th-century architectural gem, reflecting the importance placed on education.

In addition to academic learning, these madrassas played a crucial social role. They were places for debate, discussion and exchange of ideas. Students lived, ate and slept there, forming a true knowledge-based community.

Next time you're visiting an ancient city in the Maghreb, look for these historic madrasas. They will give you a fascinating insight into the cultural and educational richness of the region in a bygone era.

Fact 50 - The medina, a labyrinth of alleys

Have you ever set foot in a Moroccan medina? These historic centres of the cities of the Maghreb are like labyrinths, made up of narrow and winding alleys, overflowing with life and colour.

Each medina has its own story. Often founded centuries ago, these urban areas have retained their ancient charm, with their high walls, carved doors and barred windows. In Marrakech, for example, you can get lost in its aisles, letting yourself be guided by the scents of spices or the sounds of artisans at work.

But beyond the visual aspect, the medina is a living testimony of culture and tradition. This is where locals meet to shop, chat or simply share a cup of tea. The souks, the bustling markets, are the beating heart, where each stall offers a sampling of local treasures.

Next time you're exploring a medina, take the time to immerse yourself in its atmosphere. Every corner, every alley, will tell you a story, taking you on a journey through time and Moroccan culture.

Fact 51 - The Itinerant Poets of the Souks

Do you know these emblematic figures who wander through the Moroccan souks, reciting verses and poems? They are the itinerant poets, guardians of Morocco's oral tradition and popular culture.

These artists, armed with their powerful voices and unerring memory, share poetic, often improvised narratives that touch on love, wisdom, politics or everyday life. In the souk of Marrakech for example, you might be surprised to hear a captivating poem recited right in the middle of the crowd, capturing the attention of passers-by.

But these poets are not just artists. They are also chroniclers of society, reflecting the concerns, joys and sorrows of the people. Their poetry is a window on the Moroccan soul, a mixture of ancestral traditions and modernity.

So, the next time you visit a Moroccan souk, keep your ears open. You might be charmed by the melody of a poem, reminding you that poetry is everywhere, even in the hustle and bustle of a busy market.

Fact 52 - The Red Clay of Tamgroute

Have you ever seen this deep green pottery, typical of Morocco? These wonders come largely from Tamgroute, a small village in the South. But did you know that the magic starts long before the color green? It all starts with the unique red clay of this region.

Tamgroute clay is renowned for its superior quality. Once extracted, it is carefully shaped by talented craftsmen who have inherited centuries-old techniques. In their hands, this earth comes to life, transforming itself into dishes, tagines, or other art objects.

But it's the cooking that brings the real magic. Thanks to a special enamel, composed of copper, among other things, the red clay turns green when fired. This distinctive green hue has become emblematic of Tamgroute, and you'll no doubt recognize his works in Moroccan homes and riads.

The next time you come across green pottery from Morocco, remember the red clay of Tamgroute and the expert hands that have transformed this land into a treasure trove of art and tradition.

Fact 53 - Beaches where cows bathe

Maybe you think of beaches as places for humans to relax, with umbrellas and towels. But did you know that there are beaches where it's the cows that enjoy the sea? Yes, that's true!

In some parts of the world, especially India, it is not uncommon to see cows roaming freely on the beaches, basking in the sun and cooling off in the salty waters. In Goa, for example, these sacred animals can be spotted relaxing alongside tourists.

This cohabitation may seem unusual to some, but for locals, it is a common vision. Cows, as sacred animals in Hinduism, enjoy a certain freedom and respect that allows them to go wherever they please, including on golden beaches.

So, the next time you're dreaming of exoticism and faraway beaches, imagine sharing a moment of serenity with a cow, feet in the sand, listening together to the gentle sound of the waves.

Fact 54 - The Throne of the Lions of Ifrane

Have you ever heard of Ifrane, nicknamed the "Little Switzerland" of Morocco? This city, nestled in the mountains of the Middle Atlas, holds many surprises, including one that is particularly captivating: the throne of the lions.

In the heart of the city, in La Princesse Lalla Aïcha Park, you will find an amazing sculpture of two majestic lions carved in stone. These lions, symbols of strength and courage, proudly guard the entrance to the park, like sentinels watching over treasure.

According to local legend, these lions were carved by a German prisoner during World War II in exchange for his freedom. Although the authenticity of this story is debated, it adds a mystical aura to this work of art.

During a walk in Ifrane, take a detour to this park, and take a moment to admire these lions, silent witnesses of the history and culture of the region. They reflect the perfect alliance between the majestic nature of the Middle Atlas and human ingenuity.

Fact 55 - The Forgotten Saadian Tombs

Do you know the buried mysteries of Marrakech? Behind its ramparts and in the middle of its winding streets, the red city hides a historical treasure: the Saadian tombs. Long forgotten, they are the last vestige of a flourishing dynasty.

These tombs, located near the Kasbah Mosque, house the remains of the sultans and their families, dating back to the 16th century. For centuries, this place has been obscured, almost erased from the collective memory. It wasn't until the early twentieth century, thanks to aerial photos, that their existence was rediscovered.

The beauty of these tombs lies in their refined architecture. The precious marbles, the delicately patterned mosaics and the carved cedar ceilings bear witness to the artistic heyday of the Saadian period. The main mausoleum, with twelve columns, is particularly impressive.

When visiting Marrakech, be sure to explore this historic place. As you walk between these majestic burials, you will feel the aura and grandeur of a bygone era, but never truly forgotten.

Fact 56 - The Mysteries of the Golden Dunes

Have you ever been mesmerized by the vastness of the desert and its golden dunes stretching to infinity? These mountains of sand, shaped by the wind, hold thousand-year-old secrets. Every dune, every grain of sand tells a story.

In the Sahara Desert, especially in Morocco, these dunes take on a golden hue at dawn and dusk. This is caused by the refraction of sunlight on the tiny particles of sand. These moments are often the most sought after by photographers and travelers for their ephemeral beauty.

But these dunes are not just mounds of sand. Caravans of merchants, explorers and nomads have passed through them for centuries. Legends even say that some of these sandy mountains hide forgotten treasures, remnants of ancient civilizations or artifacts of great value.

The next time you walk on these golden dunes, think of all the mysteries they hold. Let yourself be carried away by the desert wind, and maybe you will discover one of its hidden secrets yourself.

Fact 57 - Eclipse chasers in Ouarzazate

Have you ever heard of those enthusiasts who travel the world to witness eclipses? Ouarzazate, nicknamed "the gateway to the desert", has become one of their favourite destinations. And for good reason, its clear sky offers a breathtaking astral show.

The eclipse, the phenomenon where the moon obscures the sun or vice versa, is an event awaited by many astronomers and curious onlookers. In Ouarzazate, the absence of light pollution and its geographical location make the city a privileged observation point. During these events, the city welcomes thousands of visitors who come to admire the celestial ballet.

But it's not just a gathering of enthusiasts. Scientists are also taking advantage of these opportunities to conduct in-depth studies on these space phenomena. They set up their telescopes and other instruments to capture every detail of the eclipse.

So, if one day you find yourself in Ouarzazate during an eclipse, don't hesitate to roll your eyes. You will share a unique moment with eclipse chasers from all over the world.

Fact 58 - The Olive Tree, the Thousand-Year-Old Tree

The olive tree is much more than just a tree for many crops. With its gnarled trunk and silvery leaves, it has carved out a special place for itself in the history, traditions and gastronomy of many regions. Did you know that some olive trees are thousands of years old?

It is not for nothing that the olive tree is often associated with peace and longevity. Its roots dig deep into the earth, allowing it to withstand the harshest conditions, whether drought or poor soils. It is the symbol of resilience par excellence.

In the Mediterranean, the olive tree is at the heart of many traditions. Olive oil, produced from its fruits, is a central element of Mediterranean cuisine. It is known for its health benefits, especially thanks to its richness in antioxidants and monounsaturated fatty acids.

The next time you come across an olive tree or taste olive oil, remember the tree's thousand-year-old history. It's a whole heritage that is passed on through him.

Fact 59 - The fortified granaries of the Atlas Mountains

In the heart of the Moroccan Atlas, you will discover surprising structures perched on steep heights: the fortified granaries. These buildings, some of which are a hundred years old, bear witness to a time when the need to protect crops from looters was paramount.

Built of adobe, stone, or brick, these granaries were used to store not only foodstuffs, but also valuables, documents, and essential goods. Their high-altitude position provided a natural defense, while their thick walls and strong gates added an extra layer of security.

But they are not simply functional structures. With their imposing shapes and unique architecture, fortified granaries are also true works of art. Some are still in use today, while others have become tourist attractions, attracting travelers curious to learn about this fascinating aspect of Moroccan history.

So, if one day you walk through the Atlas Mountains, look up and admire these witnesses of the past, reflections of a rich culture and a complex history.

Fact 60 - The Hidden Roman Baths

Imagine yourself, in the heart of the city, walking on the cobblestones of a narrow alley when, suddenly, you discover the discreet entrance to an ancient Roman bath. These baths, known as "baths", are ancient architectural wonders scattered throughout the Mediterranean basin, witnesses to the vast Roman Empire.

Designed for public bathing, the baths were more than just places of cleanliness. They were the social heart of Roman cities, where citizens came to relax, socialize, and even discuss politics or business. The large vaulted rooms, the hot and cold water pools, and the magnificent mosaics on the floor show the importance and refinement of these spaces.

However, with the fall of the Roman Empire, many of these baths were abandoned or were swallowed up by urban growth. But some have survived, hidden under modern streets or behind the facades of contemporary buildings.

During your travels, if you're lucky enough to stumble upon one of these hidden gems, take a moment to appreciate this open window to the distant past.

Fact 61 - The Snake Charmers of Jemaa el-Fna

Here you are in Marrakech, in the heart of the famous Jemaa el-Fna square. Between the food stalls, the musicians and the storytellers, one particular scene catches your eye: men surrounded by snakes, snake charmers, an ancestral tradition that has endured for centuries.

These performers, dressed in long, colorful robes, play the flute to "charm" snakes, usually cobras or pythons. But it's not about magic. In reality, snakes react to the charmer's movements and not to the melody of the flute. It is a game of skill and interaction between man and animal.

Despite their dangerous appearance, most of these snakes are harmless, either because they have been depoisoned or because they are naturally non-venomous. Nevertheless, the show they offer with their charmers is hypnotic, mixing mystery, fear and fascination.

If you dare to get close, you might even have the opportunity to take a picture with one of them around your neck. An unforgettable experience in the heart of the Marrakech medina.

Fact 62 - Honey from the mountains of Morocco

If you've ever had the opportunity to taste Moroccan honey, you know how delicious and unique it is. Morocco's mountains, especially those in the High Atlas, are full of wildflower varieties that give a particularly tasty nectar.

Bees in these mountainous regions forage freely among thyme, lavender and other wildflowers, producing honeys with distinct and fragrant flavors. Each valley, each altitude, offers a different taste palette, making each jar of honey a true natural work of art.

But this honey is not only distinguished by its taste. For centuries, it has been recognized for its medicinal properties. Mountain dwellers use it to treat sore throats, colds or as a natural sweetener.

If you're heading to Morocco, don't hesitate to visit one of the local markets to get your hands on this precious nectar. Not only will you be supporting local beekeepers, but you will also be bringing back an incomparable taste memory from your trip.

Fact 63 - The leather craftsmen of Fez

When you enter the medina of Fez, it's hard not to be intrigued by the characteristic smell of fresh leather. Fez is renowned for its centuries-old tanneries where the art of leather is perpetuated from generation to generation.

The Chouara tanneries, for example, are a real sight to behold. Stone vats filled with natural dyes and various liquids form a patchwork of bright hues. This is where animal skins are transformed into beautiful pieces of leather. If you look closely, you'll see the craftsmen dive, scrub, and treat the skins with impressive dexterity.

This leather is then used to make a variety of items, ranging from traditional slippers to elegant bags. As you walk through the medina, you'll discover workshops where master craftsmen shape, sew, and decorate these objects with remarkable precision.

Don't leave Fez without getting a piece of leather. Not only will you have an authentic memory, but you will also be supporting an ancestral craft that is the beating heart of this historic city.

Fact 64 - The Mysterious Drawings of the Desert

Have you ever heard of the enigmatic geoglyphs that dot some of our planet's deserts? These monumental drawings traced on the ground, visible mainly from the air, arouse curiosity and admiration.

The most famous of these, arguably, is in Peru: the Nazca Lines. But other deserts, especially in North Africa, also hide mysterious, lesser-known but equally fascinating tracks. Designed by ancient peoples, these geoglyphs can represent animals, people, or symbols.

In Morocco, for example, geoglyphs have been discovered in some desert regions. Although their precise meaning remains a mystery, these drawings bear witness to the presence and ingenuity of ancient civilizations in the face of the arid vastness of the desert.

The next time you're flying over a desert or exploring its sandy expanses, keep your eyes peeled. Who knows, you might stumble upon one of those enigmatic testimonies of the past, evoking long-lost histories and cultures.

Fact 65 - The Jinns of Morocco

Have you ever immersed yourself in the tales and legends of Morocco? If so, you've probably crossed paths with the jinn. These supernatural creatures, also mentioned in Islamic religious texts, occupy an important place in Moroccan popular culture.

According to belief, jinns, although usually invisible to the eyes of humans, live among us. They inhabit mountains, forests, deserts, and even the dark corners of homes. Some are benevolent, others mischievous or downright evil.

In Morocco, various traditional practices aim to protect individuals from bad jinns or to solicit their help. For example, during some ceremonies, healers invoke these spirits to cure illnesses or to drive away unwanted entities.

So, the next time you wander through a Moroccan souk, listen carefully to the stories the elders will tell you. They might just give you a fascinating insight into the mysterious world of the jinn and their influence on daily life in Morocco.

Fact 66 - The Hanging Gardens of Rabat

Rabat, the capital of Morocco, is not only a political and administrative center. It holds many secrets, and among them, the hanging gardens remain one of the most unknown treasures. Wondering what it is? Let me enlighten you.

In the heart of the city, hidden between modern buildings, are small havens of greenery, perched on the roofs of houses and buildings. These gardens, often seen as urban oases, offer a respite from the hustle and bustle of the streets below. The locals cultivate them with passion, planting flowers, aromatic herbs and even a few fruit trees.

These green spaces are not only aesthetically pleasing. They also play an ecological role, contributing to the thermal regulation of buildings and the purification of urban air. In addition, they are sometimes linked to ancestral practices, where the cultivation of medicinal plants occupies a privileged place.

If you have the opportunity to travel to Rabat, look up and admire these gardens of a special kind. Maybe you'll even have the chance to visit one of them and experience the serenity they offer.

Fact 67 - The Blue Diamond of Chefchaouen

Chefchaouen, often called the "Blue Pearl" of Morocco, is a unique city that transports you to a world of azure shades. Have you ever heard of its bluish alleys? It's much more than just an aesthetic choice; There's a whole story behind this very special shade.

Nestled in the Rif Mountains, Chefchaouen is famous for its buildings painted in various shades of blue. This tradition dates back to the 15th century, when the city welcomed Jewish refugees who brought with them the custom of painting the walls blue, symbolizing heaven and the closeness of God.

But beyond the spiritual, this color also offers practical benefits. Blue, in fact, repels mosquitoes and brings a feeling of freshness during the hot Moroccan summers. As you walk through the narrow streets, you will feel this peaceful and refreshing atmosphere.

The next time you look at the photos of Chefchaouen, remember that every wall, every corner, tells a story of faith, tradition and adaptation to the local climate. And if you're lucky enough to make it there, don't forget to get lost in this blue maze.

Fact 68 - The Old Lighthouse of Cape Spartel

In the north of Morocco, where the Atlantic meets the Mediterranean, stands a majestic landmark: the lighthouse of Cap Spartel. This building, which has watched over the coast since the 19th century, has an undeniable charm and a rich history that deserves to be told.

Inaugurated in 1864, the lighthouse's mission was to guide ships through these sometimes tumultuous waters. The result of an agreement between several European nations and the Moroccan sultan, it symbolizes a time when navigation was essential and Morocco played a strategic role on the route of ships.

But the lighthouse is not just a landmark for sailors. Located near the Caves of Hercules, it is part of a wild and unspoilt landscape that lets you imagine the adventures of the navigators of yesteryear. The view from the top of the lighthouse is breathtaking, offering an exceptional panorama of the Strait of Gibraltar.

If one day you decide to explore this region, don't hesitate to go to Cape Spartel. Here you will discover not only a lighthouse steeped in history, but also a strikingly beautiful nature.

Fact 69 - The Magic Flutes of the Mountains

In the mountains of Morocco, far from the hustle and bustle of the cities, hides a melodious sound that seems to emerge from the bowels of the earth: that of Berber flutes. For centuries, these wind instruments have accompanied the traditional melodies and songs of mountain populations.

These flutes, often made from reeds or wood, are the expression of ancestral know-how. Their distinctive sound evokes the purity of the mountains and the depth of the valleys. Each flutist, through his breath and his talent, tells a story, shares an emotion, celebrates a holiday or a season.

From local festivals to family ceremonies, the Berber flute is ubiquitous. It accompanies the dances, cradles the souls and strengthens the bond between the communities. For example, during the Berber wedding festivities, you will be able to hear its melody mingle with the songs of the guests.

If you go to these mountains, let yourself be lulled by this mesmerizing air. It will tell you about the history, culture and traditions of a people who have been able to preserve and enhance their musical heritage through the ages.

Fact 70 - The Warrior Princesses of Morocco

Beyond the mountains and deserts of Morocco, there are stories of powerful women, warrior princesses who have left their mark on history. These women, although often forgotten in traditional narratives, played a crucial role in defending and managing their territories.

One of these warrior princesses was the Kahina, a Berber queen of the 7th century. She bravely led Berber troops against the Arab invaders, defending her land with unparalleled determination. Her strategy and bravery in battle made her a legendary figure.

In medieval Morocco, we can also mention the figure of Sayyida al Hurra, queen of Tetouan and feared pirate of the 16th century. She ruled the Mediterranean Sea, orchestrating daring raids and negotiating with European monarchs.

If you delve into Moroccan history, you will discover that these warrior princesses, with their strength and wisdom, helped shape the country. They are a reminder that courage and determination know no gender and that women have always been, and remain, pillars of Moroccan society.

Fact 71 - The Desert Train Saga

Morocco, with its vast expanses of desert, witnessed an extraordinary railway adventure. The desert train, as it is often called, is not just a means of transport, it is a real epic journey through the golden dunes and arid lands of the country.

Begun at the beginning of the 20th century, the construction of this railway line was a monumental challenge. Facing extreme temperatures and harsh conditions, workers joined forces to lay rails on terrain that many considered impassable. Every mile of rail laid was a victory against the desert itself.

Over the years, this train has become much more than just a means of connecting cities. It carried goods, stories, dreams and hopes. From merchants to tourists, there was something for everyone on this unique journey.

If you have the opportunity to board this mythical train, you will feel the soul of this epic, each jolt reminding you of the technical and human feat that its creation represented through the Moroccan desert.

Fact 72 - Shooting Stars of the Sahara

The Sahara, this vast ocean of sand, offers a breathtaking celestial spectacle as soon as night falls. Far from any light pollution, the desert becomes the perfect setting for observing shooting stars. These streaks of light streaking across the night sky aren't just beautiful to look at, they tell a story as old as time.

Every year, during meteor showers, thousands of shooting stars cross the Saharan sky. It's a special time for locals and lucky travelers alike. Many gather, lying on carpets or dunes, their eyes raised to the firmament, waiting for this grandiose spectacle.

But did you know that these shooting stars aren't really stars? They are actually particles or small pieces of meteorites that burn up as they enter the Earth's atmosphere. Their rapid passage creates an ephemeral light, offering a spectacle that is both beautiful and mysterious.

If one day you find yourself under the Saharan sky, don't forget to make a wish when you see a shooting star. Because in this magical place, who knows? It may well come true.

Fact 73 - The Melody of African Drums

As soon as you set foot on the African continent, a singular melody seizes you: that of the drums. These ancestral instruments, carved from the trunks of trees, are much more than just musical objects. They convey stories, emotions, and are the beating heart of ceremonies and festivities.

African drums, with their complex rhythms and varied tones, play a key role in communication. In the past, they were used to transmit messages between villages. A specific set of beats could signify a birth, marriage, or a warning of imminent danger.

But these instruments are not only functional. Drums, in their various forms, are a reflection of the soul of a community. They accompany songs, dances and sacred rites. The drum masters, with their nimble hands, tell through them the joys, sorrows and hopes of their people.

So, if one day you are invited to an African celebration and the drums are playing, let yourself be carried away by their melody. It is a vibrant testimony to a rich and profound culture.

Fact 74 - The Legends of the Date Palm

Have you ever wondered where the date you may be munching on from time to time comes from? The date palm, native to the Middle East, is surrounded by fascinating tales and legends that have rocked cultures for millennia. In Morocco, for example, this tree is often referred to as the "tree of life" because of the vital importance it has in the diet and economy of desert regions.

The date palm doesn't just produce this sweet and energetic fruit. It is at the heart of many myths and legends, especially in the cultures of the Middle East and North Africa. Dates, with their natural sweetness, are often associated with generosity and prosperity in traditional narratives, as they are a valuable source of food in arid regions.

It is not just the tree that is honoured, but also its fruit that is at the heart of various traditions and celebrations. Dates, offered as symbols of welcome or eaten during sacred moments, such as Ramadan, emphasize the sacredness and vitality attributed to this food in cultures where the palm tree is king.

On your next trip to Morocco, or any other region where palm trees stand proudly, let their shade tell you the stories of past generations. Feel, through the palm groves, the echo of legends that have traveled through the ages, carried by the gentle winds of the desert.

Fact 75 - The Gates of Time in Volubilis

Have you ever dreamed of traveling through time? The ruins of Volubilis, located near Meknes in Morocco, give you this unique opportunity. This ancient Roman site is a treasure trove of history that has stood the test of time, offering a priceless glimpse into Morocco's distant past.

Volubilis, once flourishing, was one of the main cities of the Roman Empire in North Africa. As you wander among the majestic columns and preserved mosaics, you can almost hear the murmurs of the merchants, the laughter of the children, and the lively discussions of the ancient inhabitants. These mosaics, in particular, tell epic stories of gods and heroes, testifying to the cultural richness of this civilization.

But beyond its Roman splendor, Volubilis was also a crossroads of cultures. Berber in its origins, then Roman, the city even experienced a period of Christian influence before the arrival of Islam. These cultural overlays have left indelible imprints on the site.

The next time you visit Morocco, don't miss this opportunity to cross the gates of time. Walk the cobblestones of Volubilis and let yourself be transported to a world where history comes to life beneath your feet.

Fact 76 - The Secret of Pink Salt

You may have already seen this surprisingly pink salt in delicatessens or on fancy restaurant tables. This pink salt, mainly native to the Himalayas, is not just an ordinary condiment, it holds many mysteries.

This salt gets its unique color from the minerals it contains, especially iron. Unlike conventional table salt, pink Himalayan salt is often praised for its potential health benefits from these minerals. It has been used for centuries in culinary rituals, but also in traditional medicine for its purported properties.

But where exactly does it come from? The Himalayan salt mines, where most of the pink salt comes from, are among the oldest and deepest in the world. Some of these mines have been in operation since ancient times. They bear witness to a rich history where salt was once as precious as gold.

The next time you sprinkle this salt on your dishes, remember its fascinating history. Behind its captivating colour lies a thousand-year-old adventure, from the Himalayan mountains to your plate.

Fact 77 - Sand sculptures in Dakhla

If you go to Dakhla, this beautiful city located on a peninsula in Western Sahara, you will probably be dazzled by the vast expanses of sand. But, beyond this desert landscape, there is an ephemeral art form that catches the eye: sand sculptures.

These temporary masterpieces are created by local artists who transform simple grains of sand into incredible structures. Whether it's castles, animals or everyday scenes, these artists shape their surroundings with surprising precision and delicacy, relying only on water and sand as materials.

Every year, Dakhla hosts festivals dedicated to this art, where these artists exhibit their creations. These events attract visitors from all over the world, curious to see how the inert dunes can be transformed into living works of art.

When you have the opportunity to contemplate these sculptures, remember the fragility and ephemerality of this art. Every gust of wind, every tide can carry away a creation, reminding us that beauty, even if it is ephemeral, is worth celebrating.

Fact 78 - The Underground River of Akshur

In the heart of the Moroccan Rif, near the city of Chefchaouen, hides a natural treasure that few know about: the underground river of Akchour. This geological wonder is the result of millennia of erosion and tectonic movements, forming a network of caverns and tunnels under the mountain.

As you explore these cavities, you'll discover a silent world, disturbed only by the gentle murmur of the water meandering between the rocks. The light reflections on the crystal clear water create an almost magical atmosphere, illuminating the rock formations and revealing an astonishing biodiversity. Some places, thanks to the openings in the rock, benefit from natural light that offers a magical spectacle.

Many locals and guides offer excursions to discover this place, allowing you to immerse yourself in this underground beauty. If you visit the region, don't miss this unique opportunity to dive into the geological history of Morocco and live a timeless experience, away from the hustle and bustle of the outside world.

Fact 79 - The Dance of the Feathers in Marrakech

In Marrakech, Morocco's vibrant red city, an ancestral tradition has endured over the centuries: the feather dance. In the bustling alleys of the medina or in the famous Jemaa el-Fna square, it is not uncommon to come across dancers dressed in costumes adorned with feathers, moving to the sound of drums and songs.

These dancers, mastering an art that has been passed down from generation to generation, use feathers not only as adornment, but also as an extension of their bodies. With fluid and synchronized movements, the feathers seem to come to life, creating a hypnotic spectacle for the spectators. Each movement tells a story, evoking nature, birds or the elements.

The Feather Dance is more than just a performance. It is the reflection of the Moroccan soul, mixing tradition, history and spirituality. If you have the chance to visit Marrakech, let yourself be carried away by this mesmerizing dance, and you will discover a precious part of Moroccan culture.

Fact 80 - The Berber Kite

In the heart of the Atlas Mountains in Morocco, the Berbers, an indigenous people with ancestral traditions, have a unique way of touching the sky: the Berber kite. For generations, this aerial game has not only been entertainment, but also a symbol of freedom and connection with the elements.

Made from natural materials like wood and paper, the Berber kite is often decorated with traditional patterns. These drawings are not simply aesthetically pleasing: they tell stories, evoke legends or represent wishes. When the kite rises, an entire cultural heritage takes flight.

Kite festivals are expected events in Berber villages. These gatherings are an opportunity for friendly competitions, where the skill of the kite masters is put to the test. Beyond the competition, it is a moment of sharing, joy and celebration of Berber culture.

If one day you cross the Atlas Mountains, don't be surprised to see kites dancing in the blue sky. You will then witness a living tradition, a bridge between earth and sky, past and present.

Fact 81 - The Floating Oases of Zagora

In the south of Morocco, in the vicinity of Zagora, a surreal vision greets you: oases that seem to float on the horizon, verdant mirages in the middle of the golden dunes of the desert. These oases, real and vital, are the pillars of life in this arid region.

Water is a precious commodity. These oases are fed by underground springs, the result of ancient waterways that have burrowed deep into the ground. These natural reservoirs, called "khettaras", provide the necessary moisture to bring life to life in the heart of the desert. Palm trees, shrubs and small crops flourish, forming a mosaic of greenery.

For the people of Zagora, these oases are not just sources of food and water. They are social centres, places of meeting, exchange and celebration. The markets come alive, children play in the shade of palm trees, and elders share stories of times gone by.

As you explore this region, these oases will teach you a lesson in resilience and adaptation. They will show you how, even in the most difficult conditions, life always finds a way to flourish.

Fact 82 - The Dragon of the Atlas Desert

Have you ever heard of the Atlas Desert Dragon? No, it is not a mythological creature, but a real species, the Sand Agame, which inhabits the desert regions of Morocco. His prickly figure and confident gait earned him his evocative nickname.

This creature is a master of adaptation. Its spiny scales, in addition to giving it a fearsome appearance, are also functional. They allow it to regulate its body temperature in the scorching environment of the desert. In addition, its changing color camouflages it perfectly among rocks and sand.

It's not just his ability to survive in such a hostile environment that amazes. The Sand Agamea has a fascinating behavior: when threatened, it stands up on its hind legs and runs quickly to escape its predators.

So, the next time you visit the Atlas, keep your eyes peeled. You might catch a glimpse of this "dragon", a living symbol of nature's strength and resilience in the face of desert challenges.

Fact 83 - Guardians of the Mountains

Have you ever wondered who watches over the sumptuous mountains of Morocco? It is not only the steep peaks or winding valleys that make these mountains famous, but also the Berbers, often nicknamed "the guardians of the mountains". For thousands of years, these indigenous peoples have lived in harmony with nature in the mountainous regions of the High Atlas and the Rif.

Their ancestral way of life is an astonishing combination of simplicity and wisdom. The Berbers practice terraced agriculture, adapted to the rugged terrain, and raise sheep, goats and yaks, which help them survive in these harsh environments. These techniques have been passed down from generation to generation, allowing these peoples to thrive in these unrewarding terrains.

But their role doesn't stop there. Berbers also play a crucial role in preserving the environment. Aware of the importance of their habitat, they practice sustainable agriculture and actively participate in the conservation of mountain biodiversity.

So, if you have the chance to explore the Moroccan mountains, don't forget to pay homage to these silent guardians who, since time immemorial, have protected and cherished these majestic landscapes.

Fact 84 - The Gems of the Sahara

Did you know that the vast and arid Sahara, often associated with golden dunes and oppressive heat, hides unsuspected treasures within it? Among these treasures, the precious and semi-precious stones that dot this desert are of inestimable value, both financially and historically.

These gems, witnesses of past geological eras, were formed millions of years ago under intense pressure and heat. Peridot, amethyst, or rose quartz, are some examples of these jewels that can be found buried in the Saharan sand. These stones, once highly prized on ancient trade routes, were traded for other goods or used as currency.

But beyond their market value, these gems are also keys to understanding the geological history of the Sahara. Geologists and researchers are studying these stones to decipher the mysteries of how this desert formed and the climatic changes it underwent.

So, if one day you walk on the dunes of the Sahara, think of the wonders hidden beneath your feet, remnants of a distant past and silent witnesses to the history of our Earth.

Fact 85 - The Mystical Caves of Taza

Have you ever heard of the Taza Caves in Morocco? These underground formations, located not far from the town of Taza, are among the geological wonders of the country and attract visitors from all over the world. Huge and majestic, they reveal a fairytale world to those who dare to venture into it.

Discovered in the 1930s, the Friouato Caves, the most famous of them, plunge to a depth of more than 150 meters. The stalactites and stalagmites they house, formed over millennia, create a setting that is as impressive as it is mysterious. When you enter these caves, it's as if you're entering another world, where time seems to have stopped.

But these caves are not only a treasure trove for caving enthusiasts or curious tourists. They are of scientific importance. Indeed, they contain fossils and traces that allow researchers to understand the climatic and geological evolution of the region.

If you ever find yourself in Taza, don't miss the opportunity to explore these caves. They will give you an unforgettable experience, at the crossroads of nature, history and mysticism.

Fact 86 - The Earthen Fortresses of the South

Do you know the amazing earthen fortresses that stand proudly in the Moroccan South? These constructions, called "ksour" (singular "ksar"), are fortified villages built mainly of raw earth. Their unique architecture, adapted to the desert climate, makes them wonders of Moroccan heritage.

One of the most emblematic is the Ksar of Aït-Ben-Haddou, a UNESCO World Heritage Site. Its high walls and towers, built of adobe, overlook a valley and offer a majestic spectacle. Over the centuries, this ksar has served as a crossroads for caravans of merchants transiting between the Sahara and Marrakech.

These fortresses are not just remnants of the past. They continue to play an essential role in the Berber culture of southern Morocco. They are a symbol of community solidarity, designed to protect residents and their property from invasions and bad weather.

If you're traveling to southern Morocco, take the time to visit these ksours. Their earthen walls, which have stood the test of time, will tell you stories of yesteryear, bravery and tradition.

Fact 87 - The Water Wells of the Desert

Have you ever wondered how people in desert areas find water? In the vast desert, water wells play a vital role. These watering holes, dug deep into the ground, offer a breath of hydration and life in the midst of aridity.

Water wells are not simply holes in the ground; They are often the result of ancestral techniques passed down from generation to generation. These techniques make it possible to locate groundwater. As an example, the Sahara Desert has thousands of such wells, each marking a crucial point on caravan routes.

The importance of water wells goes beyond simple hydration. They serve as places of meeting and exchange, strengthening social ties between communities. The wells thus become cultural anchors, where stories, news and laughter are exchanged.

The next time you hear about deserts, think of those water wells, sources of life and culture, which remain the silent guardians of millennia-old traditions.

Fact 88 - The Magic of Saharan Mirages

Have you ever heard of mirages, those optical illusions that make lakes appear in the middle of the desert? In the Sahara, this fascinating phenomenon is common, playing tricks on travelers for millennia.

A mirage is caused by the refraction of light. In the desert, warm air near the ground deflects light rays from distant objects, creating an inverted image. For example, blue skies may appear at ground level, giving the illusion of a body of water.

Ancient caravans, guided by experienced travelers, often had to distinguish reality from mirages to ensure their survival. It is said that some, deceived by these illusions, went astray, desperately looking for a source of water that did not exist.

Today, although we understand the science behind mirages, their magic remains. If you ever find yourself in front of a mirage in the Sahara, take a moment to appreciate this natural wonder, a mesmerizing blend of light, warmth and illusion.

Fact 89 - The Golden Pen of Berber Poetry

Did you know that the Berbers, an indigenous people of North Africa, have a rich poetic tradition that goes back thousands of years? Their poetry is like a golden pen, tracing narratives, emotions and landscapes of timeless beauty.

This poetry, sung or declaimed, is passed down from generation to generation. She often talks about love, bravery, nature, but also about the challenges of everyday life. For example, a famous Berber poetess, Lalla Zaynab, evokes in her verses the heartbreak of exile and the beauty of the Atlas Mountains.

The melody of Berber words, combined with the natural musicality of the language, provides a mesmerizing listening experience. Some poems are accompanied by traditional instruments, such as the Amazigh guitar, reinforcing their emotional impact.

If the opportunity arises, take the time to listen to a Berber poem or immerse yourself in reading one of these nuggets. You will discover a rich, vibrant culture, and you will hold in your hands the golden pen of Berber poetry.

Fact 90 - Ancestral Berber Chess

Have you ever wondered where the games you play today come from? The Berbers, the ancestral peoples of North Africa, had their own version of the game of chess, long before it gained popularity in Europe and other parts of the world.

Their version, known as "Zaraq," is played on a similar board but with separate rules. The pieces, hand-carved and often made of local materials, tell a story of wars, strategy and ancient wisdom. For example, instead of the queen we know, they had the "ferz", a piece that moved differently.

This game was not only a distraction, but also a form of education. He instilled patience, thoughtfulness and strategy. The old masters of the game passed on their skills to the younger generations, thus ensuring the continuity of this tradition.

So, the next time you move a piece across a chessboard, remember this Berber variant and the incredible history of games that span ages and cultures.

Fact 91 - The Lost Palace of Moulay Ismail

Have you ever heard of Moulay Ismail, the Moroccan sultan of the 17th century? Reigning for nearly 55 years, he is most famous for his architectural grandeur and his vision of making Meknes a resplendent imperial capital.

At the heart of its many constructions was a palace, considered one of the largest and most beautiful of its time. Named "Dar El Ma", this palace stretched for miles, with huge gardens, ponds and mazes of richly decorated halls. Unfortunately, today, only a part of the stables, capable of accommodating more than 12,000 horses, remains.

During its construction, craftsmen from all over the kingdom were summoned to work on this masterpiece. The materials used were of the highest quality, including marble from Italy and precious woods from Africa.

Although many of its wonders have been lost over time, Moulay Ismail's palace remains etched in the annals of Moroccan history as a symbol of boundless grandeur and ambition.

Fact 92 - The Singing Waterfall in Ouzoud

Have you ever felt the call of nature when you heard about the Ouzoud Falls? Located in the heart of Morocco's Atlas Mountains, these waterfalls are among the tallest and most impressive in North Africa, with a waterfall that plunges over 110 meters.

The name "Ouzoud" comes from the Berber meaning "the process of grinding grain", referring to the ancient watermills that are nearby. As you approach, the gentle sound of the water evokes a soothing melody, a natural symphony that seems to sing in the ears of those listening.

The place is also a haven for wildlife, including monkeys that swing from tree to tree, offering visitors unforgettable moments of complicity with nature. Also, at certain times of the day, if the sun is positioned correctly, you could witness an ephemeral rainbow forming from the water mist.

To visit Ouzoud is not only to admire a natural wonder, but also to let yourself be carried away by an aquatic melody that seems to tell the millennial secrets of the Atlas Mountains.

Fact 93 - Morocco's Milky Way

Have you ever wondered where the best places to see the Milky Way are hidden? Morocco, with its unspoilt night skies, is a popular destination for astronomy enthusiasts. The absence of light pollution in many remote areas provides a breathtaking stellar panorama.

The Sahara Desert is one of those magical places. Far from the lights of the cities, the celestial vault is revealed in all its splendour. Looking up, you can see the Milky Way stretching out like a glittering ribbon, dotted with stars, planets, and nebulae.

Special excursions are organized, where local guides take visitors to discover these celestial wonders. Equipped with telescopes, you can dive into the vastness of the universe, approaching distant objects like never before.

In short, Morocco is not only a land of mountains, deserts and cultures; It is also a portal to the cosmic infinite. One night under the stars here, and you'll feel truly connected to the universe.

Fact 94 - The Giants of the Atlas

Have you ever heard of the majestic mountains that stretch across North Africa? The Atlas Mountains, with their high peaks and deep valleys, are often referred to as the "Atlas Giants." This is not only for their imposing size, but also for the legends surrounding them.

Among these giants is Mount Toubkal, the highest point in North Africa. Rising to 4,167 meters, it defies those who seek to conquer it. Many people undertake this climb, not only for the panoramic view it offers, but also for the sense of accomplishment.

The Atlas Mountains are also rich in history and culture. Berber communities have lived here for centuries, preserving their ancestral traditions. As you travel through these mountains, you can meet villagers who will tell you stories from generation to generation, adding to the mystique of these giants.

Thus, the Atlas Mountains are not simply land formations; They bear witness to centuries of history, culture and human adventures.

Fact 95 - The Star Shepherd

Have you ever observed the night sky in the heart of the mountains or the desert, far from the city lights? In Morocco, the celestial vault becomes a dazzling spectacle. Among the storytellers, there is a legendary character, the "shepherd of the stars", who guides lost travelers with the help of the constellations.

Tradition has it that this mystical shepherd knows every star and constellation in the sky. He uses this knowledge to carve paths in the desert, guiding caravans and solo travelers through dunes and mountains. His compass? The Big Dipper, the North Star and the other twinkling jewels of the sky.

Generations of Moroccans have grown up listening to the stories of the star shepherd, a symbol of wisdom and ancestral knowledge. These stories teach the importance of nature, observation, and the connection between man and the universe.

So, the next time you look up at the night sky, think about the star shepherd and how he used the sky as a map, weaving stories and pathways through time and space.

Fact 96 - The Hidden Frescoes of the Atlas Mountains

Have you ever heard of the mysterious frescoes in the Atlas? Nestled in the heart of Morocco's Atlas Mountains, these ancient cave paintings tell stories of a bygone era.

These frescoes, discovered in caves and rock shelters, date back thousands of years. They depict scenes from everyday life, animals, hunters, and even mystical symbols. Some scholars believe that these images were means of communication, while others believe that they had spiritual or ritual significance.

Their preservation over time is a testament to man's interaction with his environment. These works of art, often located at high altitudes, provide insight into the beliefs, traditions, and lifestyles of the region's early inhabitants.

Next time you visit Morocco, don't forget to look for these hidden gems of the Atlas Mountains. They offer a window into the past and remind us that art, in all its forms, is a universal language that spans the ages.

Fact 97 - The Treasure of the Medina

Have you ever walked the winding streets of a Moroccan medina? If not, you're probably unaware of the cultural and historical treasure it contains. The medina, an old fortified city, is the beating heart of many Moroccan cities, a witness to past centuries.

At the bend of each alley, you can come across traditional stalls, artisans' workshops or ancestral houses adorned with zelliges. These colourful mosaics, delicately assembled, illustrate the finesse and richness of Moroccan art. In a corner, a craftsman may be carving wood or weaving cloth, perpetuating crafts passed down from generation to generation.

But there's more to the medina than just handicrafts. It is also a place of life, where the inhabitants meet to exchange, pray or celebrate events. Mosques, madrassas (Koranic schools) and fondouks (former caravanserai) evoke the importance of faith and trade in the local culture.

So, on your next visit, take the time to get lost in the medina. You will discover a treasure trove of history, art and traditions, witness to Morocco's rich heritage.

Fact 98 - Wizards of the Desert

Have you ever heard of the mysterious sorcerers of the Moroccan desert? These iconic figures have long been shrouded in legends and myths, and their practices are often unknown to outsiders.

In the vast desert, where nature is unforgiving and survival is not guaranteed, many Berbers have turned to these sorcerers to seek protection, healing, or guidance. These sorcerers, called "Rqayiq" in Tamazight, are often seen as intermediaries between the world of humans and that of spirits. They use herbs, incantations, and amulets to perform their rituals.

Fascinatingly, these practices, while rooted in ancient traditions, coexist with Islam, the predominant religion of the region. Indeed, many sorcerers consider themselves pious men, incorporating elements of the Muslim faith into their rituals.

The next time you find yourself walking the dunes of the Sahara, take a moment to listen to the local tales of these wizards. You will discover a little-known and fascinating facet of Berber culture, which has survived time and change.

Fact 99 - The Lost Book of the Wise

Have you ever heard of the mysterious "Lost Book of the Wise"? According to Moroccan legends, it is an ancient manuscript that contains the knowledge of the great Berber sages, passed down from generation to generation.

The existence of this book is shrouded in mystery. Some say it was written centuries ago, at a time when the Berbers dominated vast territories in North Africa. It would be composed of scrolls detailing stories, philosophies, and medicinal techniques unknown to the modern world.

Legend has it that this manuscript is hidden somewhere in the desert, protected by riddles and silent guardians. Adventurers and scholars have searched for this treasure for years, but its exact location remains a mystery.

If this book actually exists, it could offer invaluable insight into the rich Berber history and culture. While waiting for this treasure to be discovered, the idea of the "lost book of the wise" continues to inspire dreamers and seekers, offering a captivating mystery in the sands of time.

Fact 100 - The Emerald Jewel of the Sahara

You've probably heard tales of hidden treasures, but do you know the story of the "Emerald Jewel of the Sahara"? This legendary gem is described as being of incomparable beauty, shining with emerald light even in total darkness.

According to ancient chronicles, this jewel was in the possession of a powerful Berber king, who used it as a symbol of his dominance and wealth. The emerald was so precious that it was hidden to protect it from invaders and thieves, buried deep in a secret place in the Sahara.

Time passed, and the exact location of the jewel was forgotten, surviving only in the legends told by the fireside. Adventurers have tried, in vain, to find this precious stone, attracted by its legendary beauty and the riches it could bring.

Today, the "Emerald Jewel of the Sahara" remains one of Morocco's unsolved mysteries, an enigma that fascinates and attracts those who dream of discovering its buried secrets.

Conclusion

This, dear reader, is the end of our journey through the wonders and secrets of Morocco. As you go through these 100 facts, you've traveled through time, explored faraway lands, discovered hidden treasures, and met historical figures, legendary craftsmen, and guardians of thousand-year-old traditions. Hopefully, each story has offered you a new insight into this country of immeasurable richness.

Morocco, with its majestic mountains, mesmerizing deserts, ancient cities and sun-drenched shores, is a living, changing and timeless picture. Every fact you've discovered is just a small star in the vast firmament of Moroccan culture and history. There are so many other stories to tell, so many other wonders to unveil.

But, for now, we hope that these pages have inspired you, moved you, and maybe even made you want to discover Morocco on your own. Because nothing beats the direct experience, the feeling of the place, the interaction with its inhabitants. You are now armed with knowledge to enjoy every moment.

Thank you for joining us on this journey. May your steps always guide you towards new discoveries and may Morocco forever hold a special place in your heart.

Marc Dresgui

Quiz

1) Which animal is known for its expeditions in the Moroccan desert?

    a) Camel

    b) Elephant

    c) Leopard

    d) Giraffe

2) What natural element is typical of the floating oases of Zagora?

    a) Sand

    b) Water

    c) Ice

    d) Rock

3) What are the sorcerers mainly associated with in the legends of the Moroccan desert?

    a) Engineering

    b) Magic

    c) Kitchen

    d) Fishing

4) The Ouzoud waterfall is particularly known for what?

    a) His song

b) Colour

c) Temperature

d) Its lack of water

5) What does a mirage in the Saharan desert signal?

a) A city

b) An illusion of water

c) A Giant Tree

d) A herd of antelope

6) What aspect of Moulay Ismail's palace is particularly mysterious?

a) His Disappearance

b) Cuisine

c) Its windows

d) Soils

7) Which gemstone is associated with the Sahara in local tales?

a) Diamond

b) Emerald

c) Ruby

d) Sapphire

8) What do the star shepherds seek to reach in popular narratives?

a) Moon
b) The Milky Way
c) March
d) The Orion Nebula

9) What are wells in the desert a vital source of?

a) Light
b) Water
c) Gold
d) Food

10) What are the Atlas giants often associated with in local myths?

a) Protection
b) Misfortune
c) Wealth
d) Luck

11) What oral tradition is often associated with Berber culture?

a) Poetry
b) Comedy
c) Theatre

d) Novel

12) Which game has been rooted in the Berber tradition for centuries?

a) Chess
b) Tennis
c) Basketball
d) Football

13) In which region of Morocco would one find earthen fortresses?

a) North
b) South
c) East
d) West

14) What are the Taza Caves supposed to be home to according to some legends?

a) Treasure
b) Mysteries
c) Animals
d) Vintage Vehicles

15) What is the essential element for creating hidden frescoes in the Atlas?

  a) Paint
  b) Water
  c) Sand
  d) Plants

16) Mountain guardians are often depicted as protectors of what?

  a) Herds
  b) Gems
  c) Natural Treasures
  d) Ancient Tools

17) What is the golden pen associated with in Berber poetry?

  a) Misfortune
  b) Wisdom
  c) Illness
  d) War

18) According to the myth, what does the lost book of the sages contain?

  a) Cooking Recipes
  b) Forgotten knowledge

c) Lists of Ancient Kings

d) Love Songs

19) What type of architecture is common in Moroccan medinas?

a) Modern

b) Traditional

c) Futuristic

d) Industrialist

20) The Atlas Desert Dragon is a symbol of what in the local culture?

a) Luck

b) Protection

c) Destruction

d) Renewal

Answers

1) Which animal is known for its expeditions in the Moroccan desert?

Correct answer: a)Camel

2) What natural element is typical of the floating oases of Zagora?

Correct answer: (b)Water

3) What are the sorcerers mainly associated with in the legends of the Moroccan desert?

Correct answer: b) Magic

4) The Ouzoud waterfall is particularly known for what?

Correct answer: a) His song

5) What does a mirage in the Saharan desert signal?

Correct answer: b) A water illusion

6) What aspect of Moulay Ismail's palace is particularly mysterious?

Correct answer: (a) Its disappearance

7) Which gemstone is associated with the Sahara in local tales?

Correct answer: b)Emerald

8) What do the star shepherds seek to reach in popular narratives?

Correct answer: b) The Milky Way

9) What are wells in the desert a vital source of?

Correct answer: (b)Water

10) What are the Atlas giants often associated with in local myths?

Correct answer: b) Woe

11) What oral tradition is often associated with Berber culture?

Correct answer: a) Poetry

12) Which game has been rooted in the Berber tradition for centuries?

Correct answer: a)Chess

13) In which region of Morocco would one find earthen fortresses?

Correct answer: b)South

14) What are the Taza Caves supposed to be home to according to some legends?

Correct answer: b) Mysteries

15) What is the essential element for creating hidden frescoes in the Atlas?

Correct answer: a)Painting

16) Mountain guardians are often depicted as protectors of what?

Correct answer: (c) Natural treasures

17) What is the golden pen associated with in Berber poetry?

Correct answer: b) Wisdom

18) According to the myth, what does the lost book of the sages contain?

Correct answer: b)Forgotten knowledge

19) What type of architecture is common in Moroccan medinas?

Correct answer: b) Traditional

20) The Atlas Desert Dragon is a symbol of what in the local culture?

Correct answer: (b)Protection

Made in the USA
Las Vegas, NV
25 August 2024

94401885R00066